To Mr. Louis Untermeyer, Poet —

with admiration,

Ruby Fogel

(Mrs. J. I. Lerkoff)

OF APES AND ANGELS

# OF APES AND ANGELS

## and other poems

Ruby Fogel

**NEW POETRY SERIES**

Alan Swallow, Denver

To Mary

Lizabeth

& Jack

Acknowledgments are due the following publications where some of these poems originally appeared: *Southwest Review, Voices, Southern Poetry Review, Lyric, PS, Southern Poetry Today* anthology.

# CONTENTS

## I

## II

# III

# IV

# I

## A BOWL OF WANTING

Without a definition of our joy,
we come together in a casual way
and take the manna of our come-what-way
      kind of existence.

We dip our fingers in a shallow bowl
of wanting something strange and honeyfied;
and find our wanting fed by what's denied
      yet gives subsistence.

We see the bowl's dim whiteness webbed, or cleft
with crevices — a subtle kind of blight;
somehow, the web of cracks within the white
      holds it, unbroken.

Who knows what substance might be leaked or lost
before the bowl's last breakage, if it slips?
Meanwhile, there's sweet translation on our lips
      of a word, unspoken.

# FORGIVE MY STUBBORN STAR-CROSSED YOUTH

Forgive my stubborn, star-crossed youth,
so deeply chastened from a time
I learned a lie could be the truth

and truth a lie in all but name.
May I remind you (since I must)
how iron renders steel from flame;

and deep earth — stocked with amethyst —
reveals an origin of ore;
quartz was once mere crystal-dust;

and pearl was gritty sand, before
the oyster smothered it and turned
it into a nacre-polished sphere.

Thus several lessons I have learned
derive from flame and pearl and coral:
things petrified, or dead, or burned —

but seldom from things living, oral,
or from old wisdoms well discerned.
I doubt if there is any moral.

# I COULD BE GALATEA

This is fair warning: know that I could come
to you like Cleopatra, with the pearl
hid in my breast.  (In your symposium
you then could note that every Queen is Girl.)

Or I, as Ruth, could stand against the gold
and waving wheat . . . to greet you with surprised
pretended innocence of rumors told
of love revealed, or how it is disguised.

I could be Galatea turned to flesh,
who kissed Pygmalion's hands at her release
from stone, the day he shaped the marble nipple . .

But lest, like them, love snares me in its mesh,
I warn you, in our tryst beneath the trees:
I shall be Eve, and each white breast an apple.

# A DOME OF STARS

Begin with me at this deferred beginning:
imagine that we're what we're not, that Time
unfolds like flowers in a dawn of being.
Invade the dark distortions of not seeing
the major mischief and the minor crime
were how the sense equated with the meaning.

Yet if we watched for one unknown but constant
light, simple as star-fire, fixed and cold
but burning in a blackened dome of skies
(as Wisdom is the fixed star of the wise) —
we'd learn how truth is star-like to behold;
the long light-years arriving in one instant.

# A WAY TO SPEAK

Beneath a distant star, whose faint light flared
into this secret dark, our bodies find
a way to speak: though flesh be dumb and blind
as fingers touching on a ouija-board.

Behold the future, where the darkness blooms
to flickering light-petals from a candle,
but all pale shadows stretch before they dwindle
into such dark as candle-light becomes.

Here earth's immensity draws near and close
with time all telescoped from endless space;
and as we linger — face on bitter face —
not wholly joined (not even if we chose)
      but listening, we hear earth's silence speak
      down windy wooden halls, where stairways creak.

# DREAM POEMS

I.

If ever in a desiccated dream
you should appear with blandly secret eyes
and groping hands, that somehow can redeem

our aching flesh with petty promises —
what secret journey will your hands explore,
what caverns of my mind will your calm gaze

carve from the brittle cliffs of my despair?
And will you brew me potions to restore
my body to the disembodied air?

II.  ID FROM EGO

("Two beings, ah! within my breast are fighting . . ."
                                                    — Goethe)

The dream that had delivered
my *id* from *ego*, severed:

I saw myself as pure
as a bird — or an evil-doer;
or a wave that gulped the ocean,
and licked white lips, to rush on
spitting out shells on the beach.
I saw myself as each
of these — and several more:

14

maybe a matador
shaking his cape at the bull
(embroidered, beautiful),
engraving the sliced-off ear
with bravery and fear.

How all of us are brave —
the bird, the beast, the wave!
relinquishing our terror
to the dream's unshining mirror . . .
to the *id* that I became
in the shining face of the dream:

myselves in the dark eclipse
of the self that never sleeps.

### III.  THE SPECTRUM

The violet air prevails: the stacked-up shading
rests each against the other, without weight;
the luminous light-on-light immensely fading
into a dream — too lonely, and too late.

O how the darkness flies and loses what
was light: the dim unwinding of the days
that spun around this twilight-time and place,
to teach us what we knew; to teach us that

the thing we found was lost; the thing we loved
unlovable: and all the truth we knew
false as the face that mars the moon — yet true
enough; if truth be anything believed.

## "RIPENESS IS ALL"

— Shakespeare, *King Lear*

### 1.

In that lean interval
when body devours soul,
when that red fruit would fall:
    ripeness is all.

Lacking an oracle
vague or invisible
for body or bellyful —
    ripeness is all.

But what doubt, incredible,
or faith ever fallible,
becomes core incorruptible —
    if ripeness is all?

### 2.

We spoke of many things:
but who remembers what was said —
What words, with secret whisperings
could dance like lost leaves lately shed,
still flaming-bright and whirling overhead?

The world awoke when we
saw dawn beneath denuded, sullen
quite leafless trees — when silently
we saw the leaves turn brown — the fallen
fruit that the rats had gnawed, the rain had swollen.

16

# THE FINITE EYES

The infinite wonder of our finite eyes
was the world that came awake, across our sight:
we took the morning's ordinary light
and made of it majestic enterprise:

always the world would come awake like this:
we'd hear the muted wind, and then the leaves,
and then the logic-mind that disbelieves
the wisdom of its own dark emphasis . . .

no matter how we stood there, unbelieving
in what we saw, or what had come to pass —
until, in one brief backward-look of living,
the world was caught, as in a looking-glass.

# AND IF I SAID I LOVED YOU

And if I said I loved you, would you know
        how Helen said this to a shepherd-boy
        and shook the tallest towers of old Troy,
        losing her ancient kingdom long ago:
*and if I said I loved you, would you know?*

And if I said I loved you, would you care
        how Venus — nude as pearl — was prisoner in
        a shell that clothed her in its pearly skin:
        the shell lies shattered on a beach somewhere,
*but if I said I loved you, would you care?*

And if I said I loved you, would you guess
        Penelope could weave a web of waiting
        till time Ulysses wearied of migrating,
        of Circe singing, Cyclops, wilderness;
*although I never spoke a word of this?*

And though I never said a word of this,
        if cities where we walk are Troy re-built,
        and every shell a shrine where Venus knelt
        and any space between us, wilderness:
*without a word, you then would know or guess.*

# VINTAGE

Through the gleam of valleys
                    and a river
and near the gloom of mountains
                    on the sky,
the grape grows sweeter
                    when the buds go bitter;
the vine grows stronger
                    when the flowers die.

But when the taste is tested,
                    tongues will quiver;
and while our sweet lust lingers
                    love's no lie.

# II

## THE TENDER POEM COMES

After a while the tender poem comes,
bruised by the mind, or battered by the heart,
meek as remorse, or brittle as beat of drums.

A plight, somehow, of epithalamiums
(binding together what will break apart) —
after a while, the tender poem comes.

But dulcet as morning-birds devouring crumbs,
challenged by secret chirpings, it will start
meek as remorse, or brittle as beat of drums;

or nourished on old nightmares of warted gnomes
(making a beauteous fetish of the wart)
after a while the tender poem comes.

Like night itself, is glamoured with its glooms,
immune to dark — to one last star alert —
meek as remorse, or brittle as beat of drums . . .

like love comes, flickering through dreary dreams,
the natural child of an unnatural art —
after a while, the tender poem comes
without remorse, the brittle beat of drums.

# WHERE IS THE WORLD WE WALKED?

Where is the world we walked, in stubborn dread
of glory canceled by a minor word?
Where is the pulse we felt, the voice we heard,

whose flapping semaphore, or curious code
had smaller meanings than we understood —
and larger logics nothing could convey?

What reasoning could give a name to Truth,
except a desperate one that takes no turning —
goes on forever learning, and unlearning.

## GOLD-LEAF FOR THE GARDEN

Have you, with head uneasy as a king's
(prouder than other men; more sad and wise),
some simple answer for the questionings
of my hurt-haunted heart, and inward eyes?
What subtle proverb will you speak to lead
me from an old accustomed, twisted path;
what alchemy will fix or flaw my faith
in promises old prophets have decreed?

In some enchanted garden turned to gold
by Midas-touch — or wishing-on-the-moon —
you'll find me cast into a statue's mould
and weeping in the waning afternoon:
the golden garden around me like a vision . .
transfixed forever by my indecision.

## AND IF I FIND NO ANSWER

And if I find no answer
("You never understood the question,"
   that is what you said)
        and if there now is no conclusion
("But you must come to some conclusion,"
   that is what you said)
        if I have been unquestioning
(and therefore unanswering)
        just between us
(you and me)
        what will the answer be?

        At least can't we agree
        that an unanswered question
        becomes the infinite *quest?*
So if you have lost anything,
don't look for it here;

        but if you want to find something,
this is the place to look.

# THE TEAR

Immobile,
bright as glass,
it dangles near the marrow
of my nose.

But will not fall.
Indefinite, in repose,
it trembles,
mirrors all my world
as in the miniature margin
of a mirror,
unquestioning of gravity's
old error
that keeps ripe fruit from falling.

# WHAT OF THAT SMALL GOLDEN BIRD

What of that small golden bird whose song
is heard in soundless regions of the mind;
the owl that blinks and stares — and though sun-blind,
destroys the minor bird with beak and fang?

The feathers fly as gracefully as leaves
in autumn-russets, copper, burnished blues —
but two great golden eyes with depthless views
can stare the owl down. Of course, he grieves.

# SAINTS AND DEVILS

## 1.

"Don't be afraid the dye will *stain*,"
the head hair-dresser said.
"Only the nails and hair
absorb the dye for *keeps* . . .
but never skin nor lips
nor any *living* cell . . ."

So I shall not
be Lady MacBeth, walking while she weeps
"Out out damned spot!"

Only the clean Truth seeps
inside *my* pores . . .
and without remorse
in dead hair,
in lifeless nails —
        only *there*
the ineradicable lie
prevails!

## 2.

Forgive me if I erred, being human,
    moreover, being woman —
    and you, less than divine —
tell me if I was wrong

when I, deliberately once, with siren-song
    (and with a serpent's tongue)
    denied the apple-wine
was bitter: was I wrong?

Forgive me if I erred: you know I was
    accustomed to no laws
stating that saints and devils
meet on each other's levels . . .
    *but was I wrong?*

# I SHED MY SKIN

Like a snake
I shed my skin
and thus forsake
what I have been:

a child who lost
in some confusion
life's old bequest
of young illusion:

Girl, then Bride,
then Wife and Mother:
each could hide
from one another

to find each change
of skin more haunted —
stippled, strange
and disenchanted.

Though skin outworn
must change and die,
the first self born
stays always, *I*.

When my last skin
is sloughed or shed,
will one self *then*
survive the dead?

# CONVERSATION IN THE ARK

Noah, *admit* we're lost inside the ark:
the animals are wild, with wilder eyes . . .
the lions pace and peer through drowning dark.

What if the pacing lions go berserk?
What if we find werewolves in sheep-disguise;
what will become of us, within the ark?

In closet corners, fat-cheeked cobras lurk,
spitting their forkéd tongues; a blind bat flies
into my hair, and tangles it with dark.

The children curse and quarrel: hear one remark
he thinks he might go mad — or else he cries,
wailing along with wind outside the ark.

There's only the peak of Ararat — as stark
as any iceberg! But then who denies
it's doomed to melt at last and drown in dark?

What if we're finally eaten by the shark;
the raven finds no leaf; the last dove dies . . .?
how long can we escape, within this ark,
hell and highwater and the drowning dark?

# THE ROUND OF REASON

## 1.

The visions vanish — and the world becomes
the reason why the reason was betrayed:
the mortal absolute: the sum of sums:
the whole bisected, and the half displayed.

From the navel-dot in the center, the compass points
or spreads its silver legs, nearer or farther;
might reach for something infinite as star there —
or close the circle with its silver joints.

## 2.

What was the reason, child, the sun went down
and left your day unfinished; you, forlorn?
Toys gathered rust like ruin, while your clown
that always laughed, began instead to mourn . . .

What was the reason, lovers, that you knew
the strongest love most fragile, delicate —
why did you walk the compass-line that drew
love's circle curving toward the tangent hate?

# REVOLVING DOORS

We looked into a flower's face
to find the pollen-arrowed place
that guides the bee's sweet stinging kiss
down in her private loveliness . . .

or else into a cat's wild eyes
to see his eyeballs growing thin,
then burgeoning black as nights begin.
Some things are *not* for looking in.

We looked into each other's eyes
(only eyes speak loud and clear)
to find out if, to our surprise,
Love or Hate was lurking there.

No one asked, and no one answered:
Love and Hate being closely kin,
like revolving doors, on being entered,
the one let out — let the other in.

# GOODBYE, MY LOVE

Goodbye, my love: do not confuse the fact
that elemental chance was residue
of earth, air, fire, water, and the loving-act:
whole races springing from the loins of two.

We live our lives along a precipice
where eyes of old abandoned worlds keep staring
at the ancient proud-lipped potter, still preparing
the vari-colored clays of his caprice.

But even as we lie here — steadfastly denying
the yield of earth is clay, a sterile crop
of civilizations dead, and others dying —
the potter's wheel grinds on without a stop.

# III

## OF APES AND ANGELS

I see a lonely bone-white star in
a blackened sky — and the moon foreign,
cold and scarred and barren.

I see the rootless grass gone yellow
in fields left stubble-dry and fallow;
trees rotted and hollow.

And I see again the ancient family
of man — that stood erect and comely —
who now, derelict and dumbly,

goes loping on bent wrists; or dangles
gibbering from dark . . . in mammoth jungles
of apes, and fallen angels.

# DIRGE FOR DEMOLITION
## OF OLD BUILDINGS

*(". . . the way the world ends; not with a bang,*
*with a whimper."*          — T. S. Eliot)

The meaning once was Kisses,
or skull-and-crossboned Death:
now XXX reveals that this is
to mark the spot beneath
a demolitioner's ball.
It swings now to and from
the old X-windowed wall,
an iron pendulum

marking time to kill,
striking beam and girder,
stroking brick and sill
like *loving* . . . or like *murder;*
banging wall and glass
X-times. Thus multiplying
new ways the old worlds pass
without a whimper dying.

# NO BEAUTY-MARK BUT IS A BLIGHT

("Split the lark and you'll find the music.")
— Emily Dickinson

No beauty-mark but is a blight;
all blazes burn to black or white;
the blessing can become the curse.

No knowledge but the thing we knew;
no honor without envy, too:
no drum but the elegiac

beat-beat of Time and ticking hearts;
no legend without counterparts
of moments that no mind can keep.

The surest aim destroys the mark,
shatters the skull, or splits the lark.

# FOSSIL

. . . until a face, white as a blank white sheet,
seems smiling, though somewhat oracular;
the slim hands gnarled, but fingernails quite neat;
the back, though bent, still perpendicular —

early Neanderthal, undoubtedly —
these teeth and bones encased here long ago.
Ice-ages hence, they will revert and be
herself again (the one I used to know):

one flower growing from rain-polished skull;
and both are white, and almost beautiful.

# THE LAST OF LIGHT

What is life mostly but the mystic touch
of hands, the infinite touch of eyes, the touch
of lip on glass or other lip, the thrust
    of morning pulling up a shade;

                    the dream
scorched glowing in the mind — and then gone dim?

or voice striking its note like some black bell
ringing until it rusts, and then goes mute?
but rings again — far clearer than before —
    when wind's an echo,

              and the clarion chime
speaks in the future of a distant time.

# IV

## PERHAPS SOME HISTORY

I tell you this because there are no words
for keeping silent: this was my return:
the huge house, shadowy and hushed; the clock
that ticked on calmly, having been lately wound;
the maid tiptoeing, taking in my bags
and telling me I'd been away too long.

"You know," she said, "it's rained here every day:
they say the sun had spots . . . mosquitoes ride
right on you through the door, as big as flies!"

There are no words for keeping silent: listen:
you will hear more sounds of my return:
the ice-box opening for water; the sharp
untroubled ringing of the telephone.


That was the morning. In the afternoon
the pallid clouds dissolved into the sun;
and then — too suddenly — the summer night
came stroking sweaty palms across the earth,
frog-throated, asking for another rain.

Miss Dottie sent a pie for supper, called
to share a slice herself, and told us that
Meg Diller's husband had returned at last,
forgotten prisoner of forgotten wars:
now shouldn't we all go and visit *them?*

Somehow old wars had traveled around in time
to this strange moment moulded in a mist
by tick of clocks . . . by the tick of slowing rain
falling on windows, clicking on leather leaves
of dark magnolia trees, and weedy grass.

Because it rained, we stayed home after all
and talked (when we could think of words to say):
"With all that fellow's been through, guess he *needs*
some sleep," Miss Dottie said, compassionately.

But all our talk seemed strangely commonplace:
did not include a dungeon nor a war,
much less a man who had escaped them both.

We heard the rain hit snugly on the leaves,
feeding the thirsty veins with loving juices —
as he would take his wife as bride again.

Perhaps some history will record the night.

# SILENCE

One must be silent for a while
to hear the voice of silence sing:
a distant sound, deep underground,
      of earth's mute murmuring:

old volcanoes, closed pianos,
silver-rooster lightning rods;
doors of night unhinged by morning,
      seeds escaping pods:

opalescent lizards basking,
picketing fences in a row;
webs beginning, spiders spinning
      webwards, to and fro:

fire that smoulders in red-rock boulders
burnished on the western sky;
ledges proud as Indian profiles,
      staring mountains eye-to-eye;

diamonds lately lit from carbon;
garnet, granite, marcasite;
planets turning; candles burning
      waxy white-on-white:

O mystic world, from flame unfurled,
still chained by light to the lonely sun:
through your mute mouths we may hear
      the voice of the Silent One!

# SLOW TRAIN THROUGH SUNDAY

(to be read in the dactyllic rhythm of the train)

There stand the people
that live along the track,
but our train is headed north (shall we ever come back?):

with the sunset on the left, and the swamp on the right,
    the black track
is stabbing at, and fending off the night.

The mossy glooms thicken on the bleak and barren path
of sky that overhangs an old country-church beneath.
        The Sunday-lighted steeple
        and the people
        on the grass,
        stand back
        from the track
        to let the day pass . . .

We wave to those who wave at us, in greeting and goodbye;
in that one flashing moment
they are born        they live        and die.

Though the night stands hugely at the end of the track,
        the Sunday trains
        and Monday trains
and morning will be back.

# LONG DAY'S JOURNEY OF THE ANT

1.

While we stand cringing here,
dodging the dense blue air,
the trees stand tightly rooted,
limbs rotting-bare, or fruited;

assaulted by stony clouds
falling against their heads,
grasping the acid soil
with a rooted tentacle;

poised on their own dark shadow,
like sun-dials on the meadow:
granting the sun no quarter —
grow tall, as the days grow shorter.

## 2.

Down where the dark roots grope
are cracks where red ants creep
away from the sun, to the shade
of a root-deep barricade . . .

each, with the world on his back
as lightly as in a sack;
or two of them carry together,
like Atlas, and his brother.


But who of us can guess
world-weight, or weightlessness;
or which of them has been
the mate of the lusty queen . . .

Ants bury and taste and dig,
pausing sometimes to hug . . .
but take the earth for cover,
like us, when the day is over.

# AN ECLOGUE FOR ORIGINS

One night, when the old blood-brotherness of birth
shudders in the April-early seed,
the Carolina spring comes lit by candle-cones
lifted on the new-green limbs of the pines;
    lit by the white-frosted bulbs of dogwood blossoms
        socketed in the woods;
            the dull waxy lamps of magnolias;
                incandescent water-lilies
                    shining on reflectors of bright new pools;
    and blue neon-iris
                glaring on the slopes.
Spring shines with brilliant electric energy,
        warm and fertile with light,
            incubating
        an embryonic world: waiting:
until its heart can beat and it can breathe alone.

Then pale wistaria twists at the breasts
            of fat mother-oaks;
        and through the woods, the wet-nurse pines
            pour out their milky turpentines
                to cups of tin
                    still shining and
                        unrusted.

# WILDERNESS IN G-FLAT

### 1.

I always hated the G-Flat scale.
Six flats, you know?
more flats than there are in any *other* scale,
and more flats than should be in one octave.
    Besides, how *can* you flat the C?
    There's no black key
    for that:
    so C-Flat
    is really *B* . . .
                (which, no matter what you *call*
                it, is not C-Flat at all . . .)

My piano-teacher always sat in a dim corner
    of the quick-gone Carolina afternoon.
Suddenly the November night would come,
    blotting out the day.
                *Five o'clock*
                *tick tock*

                *tock tick*
                *walk quick*
                *walk quick*
                *tock tick*

        Was it only the metronome,
        or the soft footsteps of Time itself
            walking away?

45

But in April, the day
lingered:
it would *not* go away.
At five o'clock the sun still shone,
sticking out tongues of sparkle
at the glassy face of the clock.
Outside the window,
the shadow of a bee
trembled across the sun,
made love to a shameless flower
in a scarlet gown.


In April, my music-teacher always had neuralgia.
While a maid with
licorice fingers
massaged her shoulders, she would look out
at the lonely street, where the G-Flat scale
went walking quickly, quickly.

And the metronome would say,
*"Quick quick*
*quick quick"*

## 3

But the red poinsettias always waited
    for winter:
they bloomed in February,
when all the grass turned brown.

The poinsettias were sedate:
    they did not mate
        with bees . . .
they wore trim petticoats of petals
lifted only by the indifferent winter wind.
And the trees that grew above them
    had dark leaves
    hung with moss
and winter-rotted hammocks.

I remember, I could swing
      in the torn web
of the hammock's rotting string . . .

Above
    me, in the soft dark bosom of the magnolia tree
    rocked the first white magnolias,
    cradle-shaped
with love.

# TWO ADVICES FOR POETS

## 1. *In General,*

Derive the difficult and spare and strange,
from whatever once was drab and commonplace:
not how the hearts were broken, but why they cringe:
tell off the living legend to its face.

Beat swords with poems — to ploughshares, pruning-hooks;
know wrath from complex anger, or simple rage.
Make (if you can) a mountain, tall as books,
where you, inscrutable, watch from each page.

## 2. *In Particular,*

Without a canting homily of despair,
decry whoever battens on his blood-brothers.
Take serious poems seriously; tear others
in half. Learn to distinguish what to tear.

Follow a forest: see what bird has flown
away from the tallest trees; dissect the twigs.
Find rarest fruit and eat; give him who begs
whatever he wants or begs. But sleep alone.